J.S. BACH

T0117644

ISBN 978-1-4950-4511-0

7777 W. BLUEMOUND RD. P.O. BOX 13819 MILWAUKEE, WI 53213

In Australia Contact:
Hal Leonard Australia Pty. Ltd.
4 Lentara Court
Cheltenham, Victoria, 3192 Australia
Email: ausadmin@halleonard.com.au

Visit Hal Leonard Online at
www.halleonard.com

AIR ON THE G STRING
from ORCHESTRAL SUITE NO. 3

By JOHANN SEBASTIAN BACH

ARIA
from THE GOLDBERG VARIATIONS

By JOHANN SEBASTIAN BACH

Moderately slow

Moderately fast Swing

GAVOTTE
from FRENCH SUITE NO. 5

By JOHANN SEBASTIAN BACH

Moderately with straight 8th feel

12

To Coda ⊕   Hard Swing

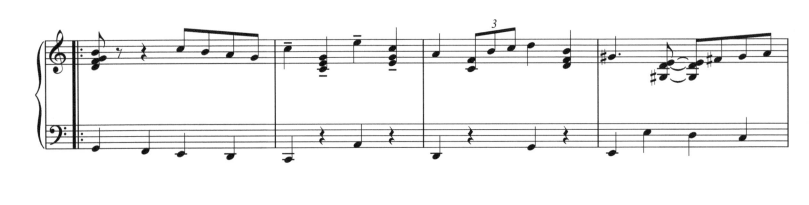

BE THOU WITH ME
(Bist du bei mir)

By JOHANN SEBASTIAN BACH

Moderate Jazz Waltz

JESU, JOY OF MAN'S DESIRING

By JOHANN SEBASTIAN BACH

Moderately

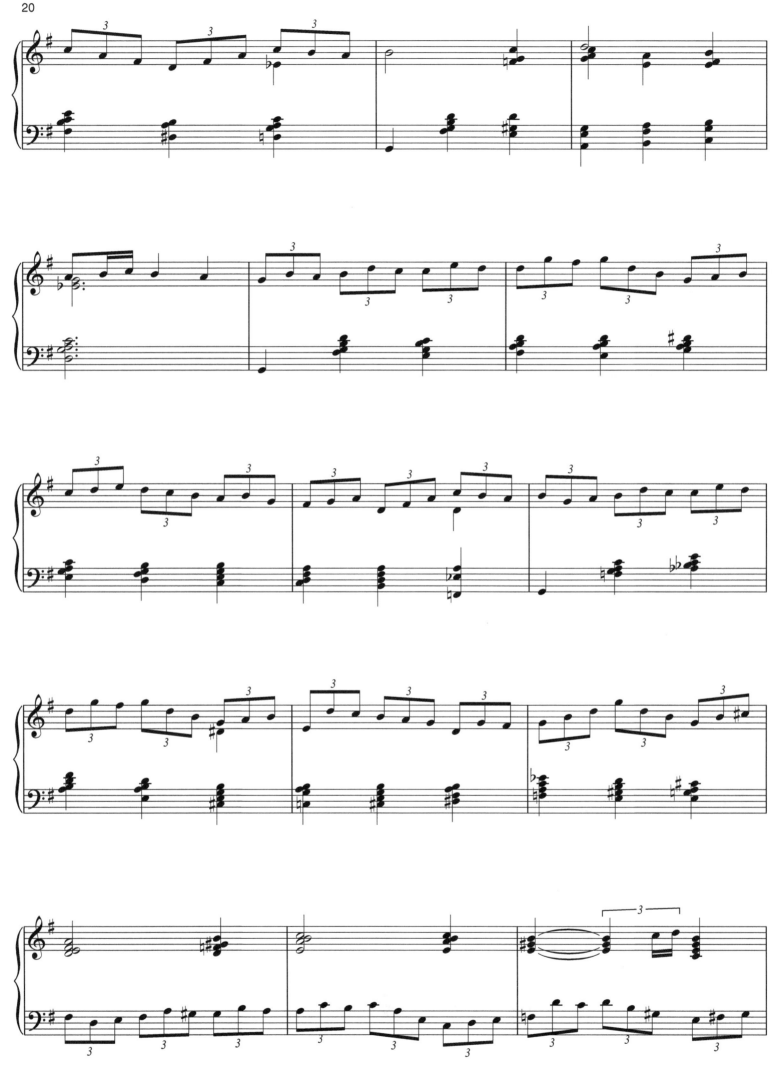

LARGO
from Piano Concerto in F minor

By JOHANN SEBASTIAN BACH

Moderately

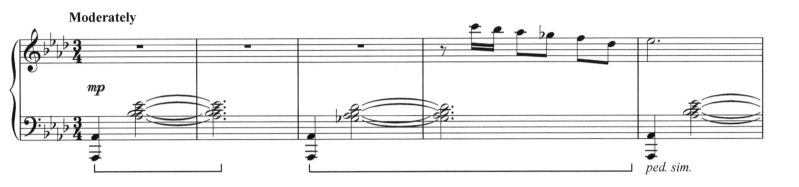

MARCH
from THE ANNA MAGDALENA NOTEBOOK

By JOHANN SEBASTIAN BACH

D.S. al Coda

CODA

SHEEP MAY SAFELY GRAZE
from CANTATA NO. 208

By JOHANN SEBASTIAN BACH

Grooving Gospel

D.S. al Coda

CODA

molto rit.

8vb

MINUET IN G
from THE ANNA MAGDALENA NOTEBOOK

By JOHANN SEBASTIAN BACH

Moderate Swing

To Coda

D.C. al Coda

CODA

rit.

MUSETTE
from THE ANNA MAGDALENA NOTEBOOK

By JOHANN SEBASTIAN BACH

Moderately fast Latin

To Coda ⊕

SLEEPERS WAKE
(Wachet auf)

By JOHANN SEBASTIAN BACH

44

SICILIANO

By JOHANN SEBASTIAN BACH

Moderately slow Swing